P9-BJC-623

The Countries

Haiti

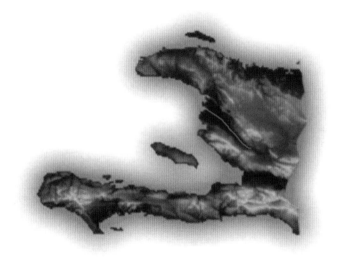

Kate A. Furlong
ABDO Publishing Company

visit us at
www.abdopub.com

Published by ABDO Publishing Company, 4940 Viking Drive, Edina, Minnesota 55435.
Copyright © 2003 by Abdo Consulting Group, Inc. International copyrights reserved in
all countries. No part of this book may be reproduced in any form without written
permission from the publisher.

Printed in the United States.

Photo Credits: Corbis
Contributing Editors: Tamara L. Britton, Kristin Van Cleaf, Stephanie Hedlund
Art Direction & Maps: Neil Klinepier

Library of Congress Cataloging-in-Publication Data

Furlong, Kate A., 1977-
    Haiti / Kate A. Furlong.
       p. cm. -- (The countries)
    Summary: Provides an overview of the history, geography, people, economy,
government, and other aspects of life in Haiti.
    Includes index.
    ISBN 1-57765-841-8
      1. Haiti--Juvenile literature. [1. Haiti.] I. Title. II. Series.

F1915.2 .F87 2002
972.94--dc21
                                                                    2002018359

Contents

Bonjou!

Hello from Haiti! Haiti is located on an island in the Caribbean (care-uh-BEE-uhn) Sea. Its land has many mountains. In fact, the word Haiti means Mountainous Land in Arawak (ARE-uh-wack), the language of Haiti's native people.

Over the years, Haitians (HAY-shens) have created a rich **culture**. Their festivals are a colorful blend of Catholic and **voodoo** beliefs. Haiti's artists have created beautiful art and music.

Despite this, Haiti has had many problems. The country has a long history of slavery. Its government is unstable. Haiti's **economy** is weak, and many of its people are very poor. Today, Haitians are working to overcome these problems.

Bonjou *from Haiti!*

Fast Facts

OFFICIAL NAME: Republic of Haiti (Republique d'Haiti)
CAPITAL: Port-au-Prince

LAND
- Area: 10,714 square miles (27,749 sq km)
- Mountain Ranges: Massif du Nord, Massif de la Selle, Massif de la Hotte
- Highest Peak: Mount la Selle 8,773 feet (2,674 m)
- Major River: Artibonite River

PEOPLE
- Population: 6,964,549 (July 2001 est.)
- Major Cities: Port-au-Prince, Cap-Haïtien
- Languages: French, Haitian Creole
- Religions: Catholicism, voodoo

GOVERNMENT
- Form: Elected government
- Head of State: President
- Head of Government: Prime minister
- Flag: Two horizontal bands of blue and red with Haiti's coat of arms in the center
- Nationhood: January 1, 1804

ECONOMY
- Agricultural Products: Coffee, mangoes, sisal, cacao, sugarcane, rice, corn, sorghum
- Mining Products: Bauxite, gold, copper
- Manufactured Products: Baseballs, clothing, footwear, electronics, flour, cement, sugar
- Money: Gourde (1 gourde = 100 centimes)

Haiti's Flag

Women exchanging gourdes for bread

Timeline

2600 B.C.	First settlers arrive on Hispaniola
A.D. 700	Taino have established their culture on Hispaniola
1492	Christopher Columbus arrives on Hispaniola
1697	France gains control of the western third of Hispaniola; names colony Saint-Dominique
1791	Slaves rebel against French rule in Saint-Dominique
1804	Slaves declare independence from France; Saint-Dominique is renamed Haiti
1915-1934	U.S. troops occupy Haiti
1937	Dominican Republican troops murder thousands of Haitians
1957	François Duvalier becomes president
1990	Haiti holds its first free elections
1991	Military overtakes the government
1994	Military steps down, president in control of government
2001	Jean-Bertrand Aristide elected president

History

Columbus lands on Hispaniola

Haiti is on the island of Hispaniola (hiss-puh-NYO-luh). The island's first settlers arrived thousands of years ago. The Taino (TIE-no), a group of Arawak Indians, were the last to settle on Hispaniola before the Europeans arrived.

Christopher Columbus landed on Hispaniola in 1492. He claimed the island for Spain. Europeans then began settling the land.

European settlement hurt the Taino. Many died from mistreatment and European diseases. Fifty years after the Europeans arrived, nearly all of the Taino people on Hispaniola had died.

Spain controlled Hispaniola. But the French began settling the western end of the island. They established plantations there.

In 1697, France officially gained control of the western third of Hispaniola. France named its new colony Saint-Dominique (saynt DA-min-eek). Spain retained control of the other side of the island. They named their side the Dominican Republic.

A sugar plantation on Hispaniola

The French plantations prospered. Plantation owners grew indigo, coffee, sugar, and cotton. They brought Africans to Saint-Dominique to work on the plantations as slaves.

The slaves **rebelled** in 1791. They declared independence from France in 1804. Saint-Dominique was renamed Haiti. **Civil wars** soon tore the new country apart. The fighting caused many changes in leadership.

In 1915, troops from the United States took control of Haiti. The U.S. said it did this to help Haiti's people. But many Haitians believed the U.S. only wanted to build a military base on the island. The U.S. troops left Haiti in 1934.

Haiti continued to face problems. Its government was weak. Citizens held strikes against Haiti's leaders. And in 1937, troops from the Dominican Republic murdered thousands of Haitians living on the border.

In 1957, François Duvalier (fran-SWAH duh-VAL-yay) became president. He was a **dictator**. Duvalier used violence to silence anyone who disagreed with him. He ruled Haiti until his death in 1971. Before he died, he

François Duvalier standing behind his son Jean-Claude

appointed his son, Jean-Claude Duvalier (zhon-CLAWD duh-VAL-yay), as Haiti's next leader. Jean-Claude ruled until 1986.

Haiti held its first free elections in 1990. The people elected Jean-Bertrand Aristide (zhon-BURR-trand ah-ree-STEED) as president. But the military overthrew Aristide a few months after he took office.

Nations around the world disagreed with the military takeover. They stopped sending aid to Haiti. Life became very difficult for Haitians. Many fled to the U.S. looking for a better life.

In 1994, Haiti's military agreed to step down. Aristide regained his title as president. In 1996, René Préval (RAH-nay PRAY-val) was elected president. Aristide was again elected president in 2001.

Today, Haiti faces challenges. Many of its people are poor. The **economy** is weak, and the government is still unstable. Haitians are pulling together to strengthen their country for the future.

Jean-Bertrand Aristide was sworn in for his second term as Haiti's president on February 7, 2001. Senate President Yvon Neptune looks on.

The Land

Haiti's land covers the western third of Hispaniola. This island lies between the Caribbean Sea and the Atlantic Ocean. Haiti shares the island with the Dominican Republic.

Haiti has a long coastline with two **peninsulas**. The Gulf of Gonâve (go-NAHV) separates the peninsulas. Rocky cliffs surround much of Haiti's coasts. But there are also several **accessible** harbors.

Haiti's mountainous land

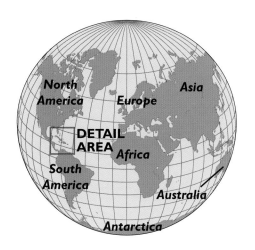

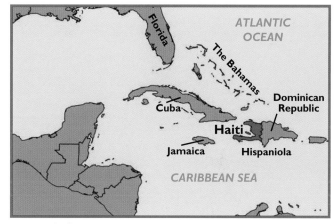

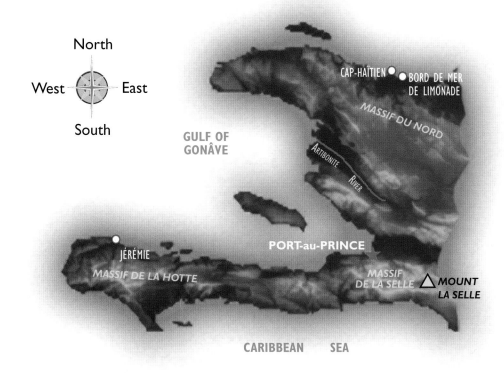

Many mountains rise from Haiti's land. Mount la Selle (MOWNT la SAY-lay), in southeastern Haiti, is the country's highest peak. Plains lie between the mountain ranges. Haitians use these fertile plains for farming.

Haiti has a warm, tropical climate. The average temperatures range from 70 to 90°F (21 to 32°C). The warmest months are July and August. The coolest months are December through March.

Haiti has two rainy seasons. One occurs in the spring, the other occurs in the fall. During these times, Haiti's rivers might flood. But during the dry season, many of Haiti's rivers can become completely dry.

Hurricanes threaten Haiti's shores from August through October. These storms have high winds and heavy rains. Some hurricanes have the power to sweep away entire towns, destroy bridges and roads, and wipe out crops.

Rainfall

Rain

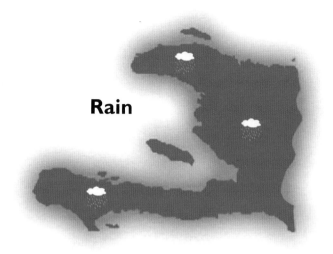

AVERAGE YEARLY RAINFALL

Inches		*Centimeters*
Under 40		*Under 100*
40 - 60		*100 - 150*
Over 60		*Over 150*

North
West — East
South

Temperature

AVERAGE TEMPERATURE

Fahrenheit		*Celsius*
Over 70°		*Over 21°*
50° - 70°		*10° - 21°*
30° - 50°		*-1° - 10°*

Summer/Winter

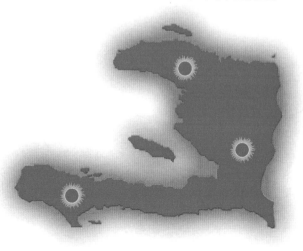

Plants & Animals

Haitians have cleared many of the plants in their country. They did this to create fields for their crops and grazing areas for their livestock. They also cut down trees to use as timber. Despite this, native plants still grow in Haiti.

Mesquite trees can grow to be 50 feet (15 m) tall.

Orange, lime, avocado, mango, and palm trees grow wild in Haiti. Pine trees, ferns, and orchids grow on Haiti's mountain slopes. Mangrove trees grow along the coasts. Cacti and mesquite trees grow well in Haiti's dry areas.

Haiti's plants provide homes for many animals. More than 300 bird species live in the country. One of Haiti's most common birds is the palm-chat. It is a large, brown songbird. The palm-chat lives in the tops of palm trees.

Haiti is also home to other animals. Caiman (KAY-mun) are animals that look like crocodiles. They live in southern Haiti. Lobsters, turtles, and crayfish live in Haiti's coastal waters.

The speckled caiman eats fish, amphibians, reptiles, and water birds. Because they eat so many fish, caimans help keep Haiti's piranha population under control.

Haitians

About seven million people live in Haiti. Nearly all of these people are **descendants** of African slaves. A small number of **mulattos** and whites also live in Haiti.

Haiti's official languages are French and Haitian Creole (KREE-ole). The upper class speaks French. But most of the people speak Haitian Creole. It is a mix of French, Spanish, and African languages.

The majority of Haitians are Roman Catholic. It is Haiti's official religion. Many Haitians believe in **voodoo**, too. It is a religion that mixes Catholic saints, African gods, and magical elements.

Most Haitians are peasants. They live in the country and work as farmers. They usually live in small, wooden houses. These houses often do not have electricity or running water. Women usually cook food outside on open fires.

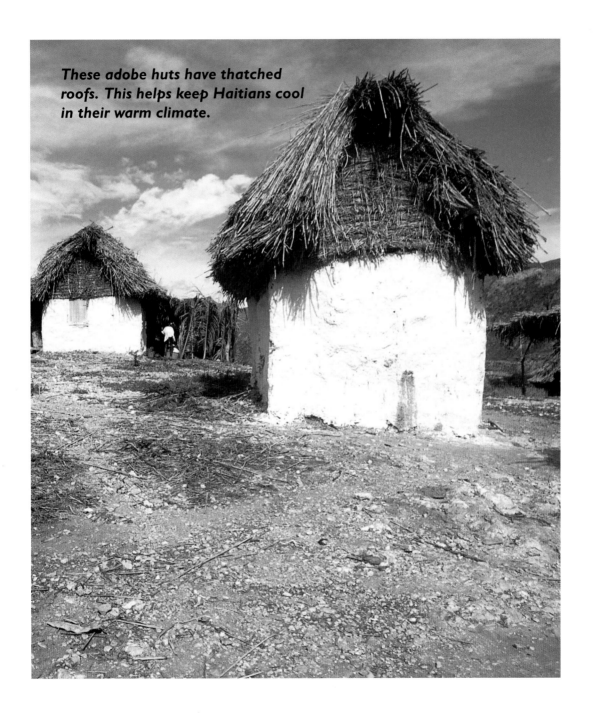

These adobe huts have thatched roofs. This helps keep Haitians cool in their warm climate.

Haiti's small upper class lives much differently than the peasants. Many members of the upper class live in Haiti's largest cities. These people often own their own mansions. The mansions have high walls for privacy and protection.

Haitians eat a variety of foods. Pumpkin soup is one of Haiti's specialties. Cornmeal mush cooked with kidney beans, peppers, and coconut is another popular meal. Rice, beans, and fried plantains are also common foods.

The Haitian government provides free public education. Haiti's laws state that children between the ages of 7 and 13 must attend school. But uniforms and books are costly. And few schools are located in the countryside. So less than half of all Haitian children attend school.

French is taught in most schools and in written lessons. But primary school students are taught in the Haitian Creole language. It is the language most commonly spoken among Haitian peasants.

Haitians often cook over open fires.

Beyen

Fried Bananas

- 3 ripe bananas
- 1 tablespoon flour
- 1/4 teaspoon cinnamon

- 1/2 teaspoon vanilla extract
- 1 tablespoon sugar
- 1/8 tablespoon baking soda

Mash bananas in a medium bowl. Add flour, cinnamon, vanilla, sugar, and baking soda to the mashed bananas and mix together. With an adult's help, place spoonfuls of the batter into hot oil. Fry until golden brown. Sprinkle with sugar and serve. Serves three.

AN IMPORTANT NOTE TO THE CHEF: Always have an adult help with the preparation and cooking of food. Never use kitchen utensils or appliances without adult permission and supervision.

English	Haitian Creole
Hello _____	Bonjou (BOH-jyou)
Please _____	Silvouple (SEEL-voo-play)
Thanks _____	Gras (GRAHS)
Girl _____	Tifi (TEE-fee)
Boy _____	Gason (gas-SOH)
Friend _____	Zanmi (ZAN-mee)

LANGUAGE

The Economy

A majority of Haitians are farmers. They have small farms in the countryside. Their main crops are rice, corn, beans, and fruits. But because their farms are so small, they often grow just enough food for their own families.

People who own larger farms grow crops to export. Coffee is Haiti's major export crop. Other important crops are sugarcane, sisal, and cacao.

The Port-au-Prince (port-oh-PRINTS) area has many factories. People who work there manufacture goods. These goods include electronics, baseballs, and clothing.

Some people also work as miners. They dig up minerals such as **bauxite**, copper, and gold. Haiti imports other minerals, such as coal and **petroleum**. They are used as energy sources. Haiti also gets energy from **hydroelectric** power.

Opposite page: Haitian art is also an important part of trade. This art dealer has set up a display on the beach to sell paintings to tourists.

Historic Cities

Port-au-Prince is in southern Haiti along the Gulf of Gonâve. It is Haiti's capital and largest city. About two million people live there.

Port-au-Prince has much to offer. Its museums display works by local artists. The Iron Market offers shoppers everything from spices to sequined **voodoo** flags. The Institut Français (IN-sti-too FRAN-say) holds concerts, lectures, and other **cultural** events.

The city of Cap-Haïtien (kap-HAY-shun) is on Haiti's northern coast. Over the years, this city has survived three major fires, a slave uprising, an earthquake, and a **hurricane**. Today, about 100,000 people live there. It is Haiti's second-largest city.

Just east of Cap-Haïtien is the small village of Bord de Mer de Limonade (BORD day MARE day LEE-moe-naide). Scientists believe this is the site of La Navidad (la NAH-vee-dahd). It was the first fort Europeans built in the New World. They built the fort from the remains of Columbus's sunken ship, the *Santa María*.

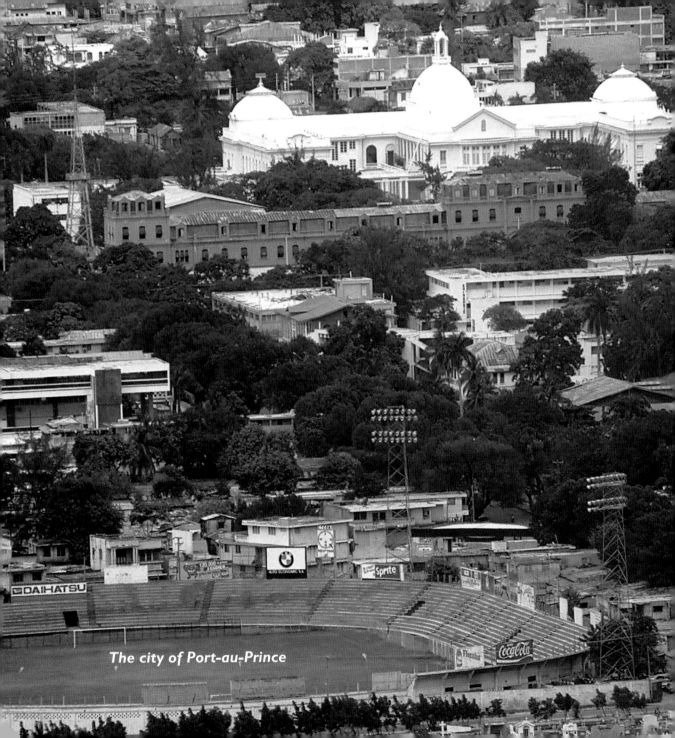

The city of Port-au-Prince

Transportation

Riding the bus is a common way to travel in Haiti. Some of the buses are old school buses. Others are trucks that have been converted into buses. These brightly decorated trucks are called *taptaps*.

Haitians also travel in taxis called *publiques* (PUB-leeks). Red ribbons hang from the mirrors in *publiques*. The red ribbons let people know the car is a taxi. People hail *publiques* by standing near the street and saying, "Psst!"

Boats **ferry** people from Port-au-Prince west to the city of Jérémie (ZHER-eh-may). Other boats transport people to Haiti's islands in the Gulf of Gonâve. Harbors in Port-au-Prince and Cap-Haïtien handle Haiti's trade.

Haiti's largest airport is in Port-au-Prince. Some flights carry passengers to and from cities in Haiti. Other flights take people to the Americas, European countries, and islands in the Caribbean.

Opposite page: On market day the streets are often crowded with people, taptaps, and publiques.

The Government

In 1987, Haitians approved a new **constitution**. It was based on the U.S. and French constitutions. Today, Haiti's government still follows its laws.

The 1987 Constitution contains many **safeguards**. For example, military officers cannot be elected to public office. And the president can only serve one five-year term. Haitians hope these safeguards will prevent a **dictator** from taking over their country again.

Haitians elect their president. The president appoints a **prime minister**. The prime minister is chosen from the party that holds the most seats in **parliament**.

Haiti's parliament has two houses. The lower house is called the Chamber of Deputies. It has 83 members. The upper house is called the Senate. It has 27 members. All parliament members are elected by the people.

The Haitian presidential palace is located in Port-au-Prince.

Holidays & Festivals

Since many Haitians are Catholic, they celebrate Christian holidays. Christmas, Easter, and saints days are all holidays. Haitians also honor their **voodoo** beliefs with **pilgrimages**.

Carnival is one of Haiti's major festivals. It takes place several weeks before Easter. During Carnival, people wear costumes. They also watch street theater and listen to live music.

Just after Carnival, Haitians celebrate Rara. It takes place the week before Easter. Bands walk along Haiti's roads playing music. Musicians play trumpets made of bamboo and tin. They play drums, maracas, and metal scrapers, too.

Many Haitians also make voodoo pilgrimages to holy places. There, they worship voodoo spirits in different ways. For Saut d'Eau (SAW DAY-ah), people bathe in a sacred waterfall and attend a mass. To honor Ogou Ferraille (OGOO FAYR-reel), people perform ceremonies and take mud baths.

Haitians celebrate with parades and music.

Sports & Culture

Sports are popular in Haiti. Many people enjoy watching and playing soccer. They also enjoy watching cockfights. Nearly every town has a cockfighting pit. Many people bet on the fights.

Haitians have created a rich **culture**. Their art has gained international fame. One of the country's most famous artists is Hector Hyppolite (EHK-tore YIP-po-leet). He was a **voodoo** priest. Hyppolite's visions and dreams inspired many of his paintings.

Racine music is also an important part of Haiti's culture. This music is a blend of voodoo rhythms and jazz. During Haiti's political unrest in the 1980s, *racine* music often demanded change.

Haiti's beautiful land also adds to its culture. People dive in the clear waters along Haiti's shores. They hike through the mountains to see cloud forests and limestone caves. Or they bird-watch to catch a glimpse of Haiti's beautiful birds.

Diving for shells is easy in the clear waters of Haiti.

Glossary

accessible - easy to reach, enter, or approach.

bauxite - the mineral that is the chief ore of aluminum.

civil war - a war between two groups in the same country.

constitution - the laws that govern a country.

culture - the customs, arts, and tools of a nation or people at a certain time.

descendant - a person who comes from a particular ancestor or group of ancestors.

dictator - a ruler who has complete control and usually governs in a cruel or unfair way.

economy - the way a nation uses its money, goods, and natural resources.

ferry - to carry people or things across a body of water in a boat or other craft.

hurricane - a tropical storm with high winds, rain, thunder, and lightning.

hydroelectricity - the kind of electricity produced by water-powered generators.

mulatto - a person who is of mixed white European and black African ancestry.

parliament - the highest lawmaking body of some governments.

peninsula - land that sticks out into water and is connected to a larger land mass.

petroleum - a thick, yellowish-black oil. It is the source of gasoline.

pilgrimage - a journey to a holy place.

prime minister - the highest-ranked member of some governments.

rebel - to disobey an authority or the government.

safeguard - a rule or law that is used to guard, protect, or defend.

voodoo - a set of mysterious religious rites characterized by a belief in sorcery and the power of charms. It originated in West Africa.

Web Sites

Would you like to learn more about Haiti? Please visit **www.abdopub.com** to find up-to-date Web site links about Haiti's art, history, and wildlife. These links are routinely monitored and updated to provide the most current information available.

Index